SCIENCE KIDS
Life Cycles

Salmon

Ruth Daly

LET'S READ AV2 BY WEIGL™
ADDED VALUE • AUDIO VISUAL

Go to **www.av2books.com**, and enter this book's unique code.

BOOK CODE

U134935

AV² by Weigl brings you media enhanced books that support active learning.

AV² provides enriched content that supplements and complements this book. Weigl's AV² books strive to create inspired learning and engage young minds in a total learning experience.

Your AV² Media Enhanced books come alive with...

Audio
Listen to sections of the book read aloud.

Video
Watch informative video clips.

Embedded Weblinks
Gain additional information for research.

Try This!
Complete activities and hands-on experiments.

Key Words
Study vocabulary, and complete a matching word activity.

Quizzes
Test your knowledge.

Slide Show
View images and captions, and prepare a presentation.

... and much, much more!

Published by AV² by Weigl
350 5th Avenue, 59th Floor New York, NY 10118
Websites: www.av2books.com   www.weigl.com

Library of Congress Control Number: 2014941063

ISBN 978-1-4896-1334-9 (hardcover)
ISBN 978-1-4896-1335-6 (softcover)
ISBN 978-1-4896-1336-3 (single user eBook)
ISBN 978-1-4896-1337-0 (multi-user eBook)

Printed in the United States of America in North Mankato, Minnesota
1 2 3 4 5 6 7 8 9 0 18 17 16 15 14

052014
WEP220514

Project Coordinator: Jared Siemens
Art Director: Terry Paulhus

Weigl acknowledges Getty Images as the primary image supplier for this title.

SCIENCE KIDS
Life Cycles
Salmon

CONTENTS

4

All fish begin life, grow, and make more fish. All fish will die in the end. New fish grow up to take their place. This is a life cycle.

Salmon live in water. They have scales, fins, and gills. Salmon can breathe under the water with their gills.

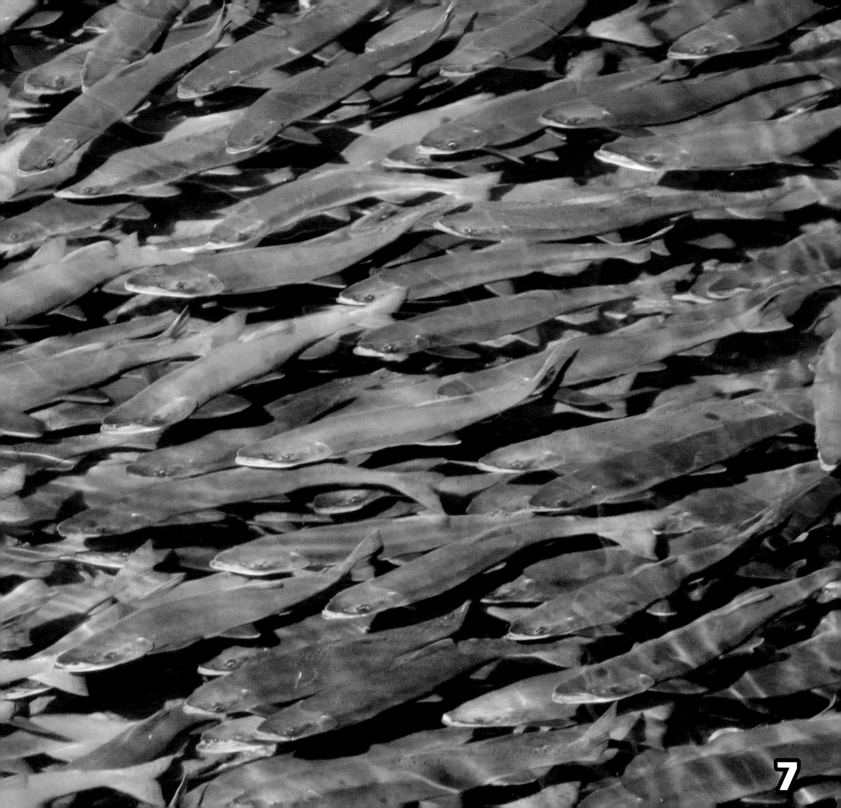

7

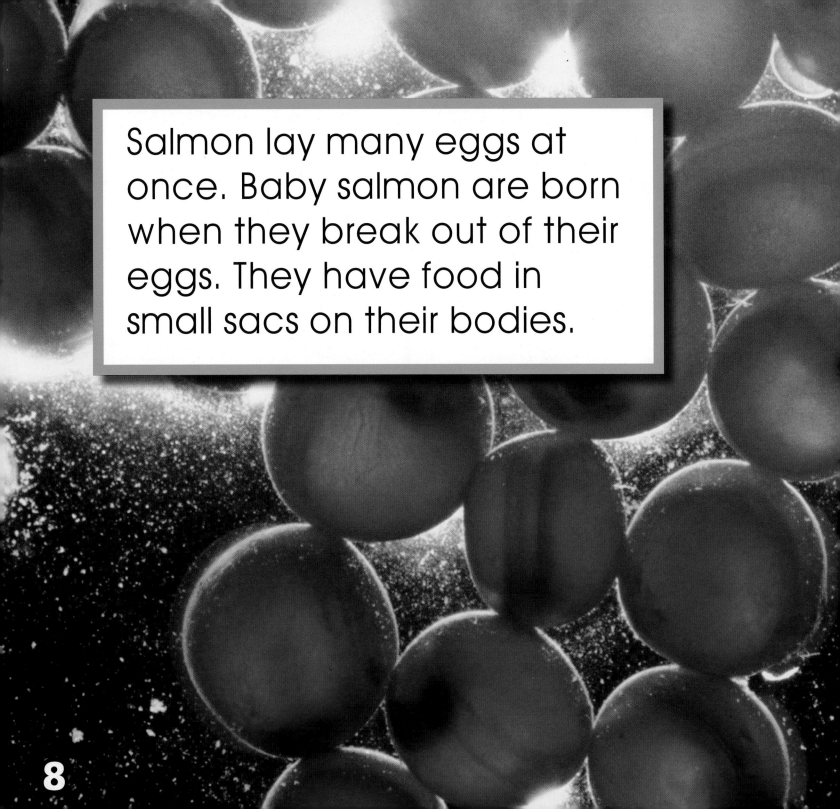

Salmon lay many eggs at once. Baby salmon are born when they break out of their eggs. They have food in small sacs on their bodies.

9

The baby salmon eats all of the food in its sac first. Then it must find insects to eat. This is the fry stage of the life cycle. Fry can move very fast. They live in rivers.

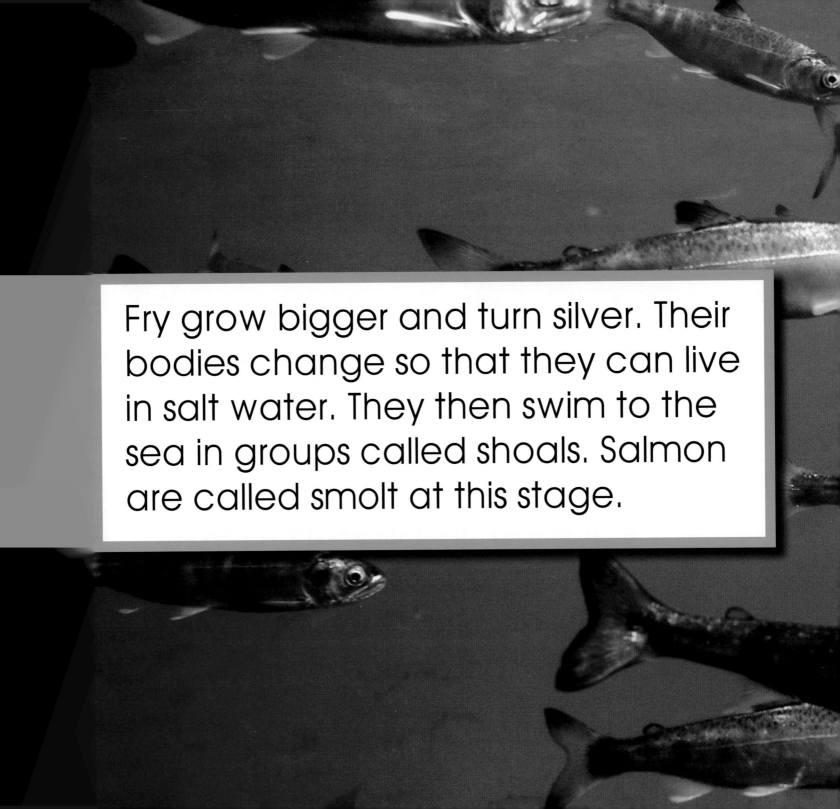

Fry grow bigger and turn silver. Their bodies change so that they can live in salt water. They then swim to the sea in groups called shoals. Salmon are called smolt at this stage.

13

Fully-grown salmon live in the sea for many years. This is the adult stage of the life cycle.

Adult salmon swim back to the river where they were born. They do this so they can lay their eggs in a safe place. This is the spawning stage of the life cycle.

17

The mother uses her tail to make a nest in the riverbed. This is where she lays her eggs. Salmon eggs are round, soft, and very small.

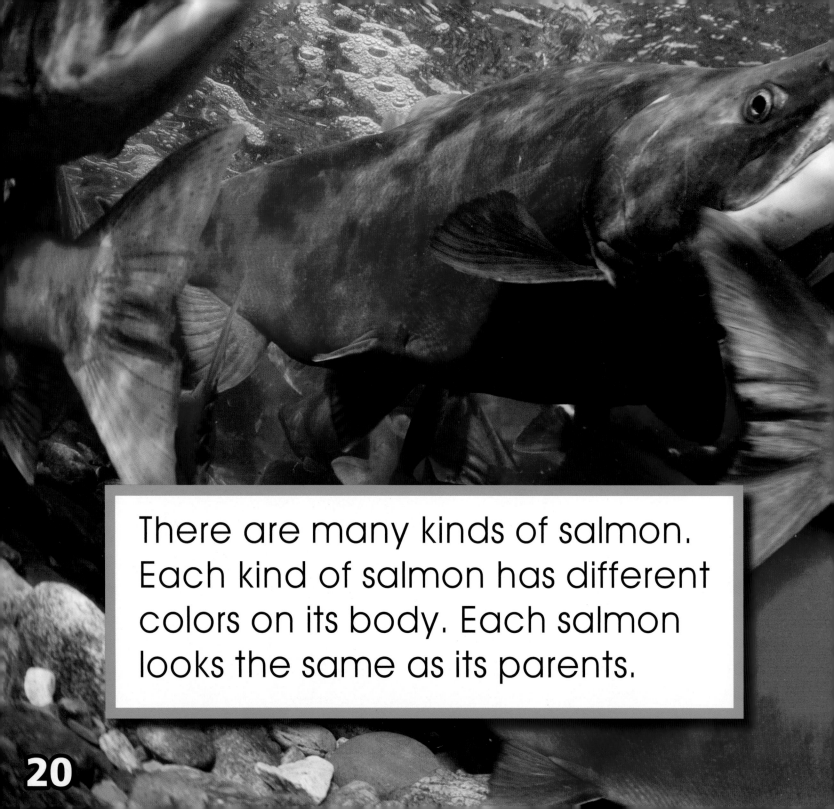

There are many kinds of salmon. Each kind of salmon has different colors on its body. Each salmon looks the same as its parents.

Life Cycles Quiz

Test your knowledge of salmon life cycles by taking this quiz. Look at these pictures. Which stage of the life cycle do you see in each picture?

egg   spawning
adult   fry

23

KEY WORDS

Research has shown that as much as 65 percent of all written material published in English is made up of 300 words. These 300 words cannot be taught using pictures or learned by sounding them out. They must be recognized by sight. This book contains 66 common sight words to help young readers improve their reading fluency and comprehension. This book also teaches young readers several important content words, such as proper nouns. These words are paired with pictures to aid in learning and improve understanding.

Page	Sight Words First Appearance
5	a, all, and, end, grow, in, is, life, make, more, the, this, will
6	can, have, live, their, they, under, water
8	are, at, food, many, of, on, once, out, small, when
11	eats, find, first, it, its, move, must, rivers, then, to, very
12	change, groups, sea, so, that
15	for, years
16	back, do, place, were, where
19	her, mother, she, uses
20	as, different, each, has, kinds, looks, same, there, these

Page	Content Words First Appearance
5	fish, life cycle
6	fins, gills, salmon, scales
8	bodies, eggs, sacs
11	insects, fry
12	shoals, silver
15	adult stage
16	spawing stage
19	nest, riverbed, tail
20	body, colors, parents

Check out www.av2books.com for activities, videos, audio clips, and more!

1 Go to www.av2books.com.

2 Enter book code. U 1 3 4 9 3 5

3 Fuel your imagination online!

www.av2books.com